Outside Magic

Also by Noah Leznoff:
Why We Go to Zoos

Outside Magic

poetry by
Noah Leznoff

INSOMNIAC PRESS

Edited by Paul Vermeersch
Copy edited by Adrienne Weiss
Cover Design by Mike O'Connor
Interior Design by Marijke Friesen

National Library of Canada Cataloguing in Publication Data

Leznoff, Noah
Outside magic : poems / by Noah Leznoff.

ISBN 1-894663-42-X

I. Title.

PS8573.E996O9 2003   C811'.54   C2003-
900707-3
PR9199.3.L474O9 2003

The publisher gratefully acknowledges the support of the Canada Council, the Ontario Arts Council and the Department of Canadian Heritage through the Book Publishing Industry Development Program. We acknowledge the support of the Government of Ontario through the Ontario Media Development Corporation's Ontario Book Initiative.

Printed and bound in Canada

Insomniac Press
192 Spadina Avenue, Suite 403
Toronto, Ontario, Canada, M5T 2C2
www.insomniacpress.com

THE CANADA COUNCIL | LE CONSEIL DES ARTS
FOR THE ARTS | DU CANADA
SINCE 1957 | DEPUIS 1957

ONTARIO ARTS COUNCIL
CONSEIL DES ARTS DE L'ONTARIO

Acknowledgements:

Some of the poems here (or versions of them) have appeared in the following publications:

Queen Street Quarterly , *The Writing Space Journal* , *Carousel Twelve* (University of Guelph), *Door of the Morning* (UnMon America), *Sing for the Inner Ear* (UnMon America), *The IV Lounge Reader* (Insomniac Press), and *I Want to Be the Poet of your Kneecaps* (Black Moss Press).

This book was supported by a Works In Progress grant from the Ontario Arts Council.

Language wears tree ears and a false moustache
For the moment. For whom? For the *moment*.

—Don McKay, *Vis à Vis*

Table of Contents

Sleeping In the Grass

Kiss me Laura, but not on the mouth
your flowering hickey, my nipple

an upturned face in the circle
with no centre; astride the permian

moss, mouldering stump, blue blossoms
observe our bed; midges loiter

in this open-mouthed rale.
O dream-heart, fiddler crab, you

artless giving in, giving out!
Leave us now with leaf-stem,

bone braided in our thinning hair.
A damselfly, I swear it, left

her string of jelly under
my tongue, beside the pebble

a jackdaw brought, plucked
from the salmon-eyed rill.

Palliative Care

The opposing paradigm proposes that the essential unit of nature is not species,
but DNA. . . . Since we think ecology is designed to create and adapt to DNA
changes—indeed it may be ecology's entire purpose—people are unlikely to do
any great harm.
   —Editorial about the bio-tech industry, *Globe and Mail,*
   June 6, 2000

What turns in the womb
a collison of planetary atoms

the arbitrary missing digit,
 nine-section citrus bulging
from calyx to stigma

here's brain, another insect-seething
 nest, telluric congress of bees
swallows flinging themselves

 to the marginal banyan
(o its knotted Aristotelian
 trick of branching rootward
to our kingdom of nerves

 and somewhat under moss, the larval
gem an out-spilling
 tremulous jelly we

 in the rock of half-life,
clicking pawl, municipal circuit
board, touch

❖

up an elevator
an earth-slinking dog
O
osmatic terrier!
   you and the various light through the
various windows, *taxis,*
  sister ports in the vein,
   once-pelagic blood, and tang
and rudiment of simmering
cabbage-tomato soup

   —I mean
a small room

a spoon
   a book like a lake
in the hands

hysterical fool,

she said, taking
him into her mouth,

there is no One

Dr. Yu

Dr. Yu, you are so
  beautiful it's im-
possible
for me not to eroticize
  pain,
masquerading,
your eyes above the surgical
  mask; what with us nose
to nose in this
  inch-intimate business,
you must know I'm crazy
  (nudging small implication
modesty fluttering)
for this digging under
the nerves of me,
  your small bronze
hand, rubbered,
in my mouth.

  We've made
pleasantries of our children,
and already I've almost
told you
a hundred times in
that minute that
your skin—
  that I need
no anaesthetic, just
  a full-grown mind
  and
you
  Yu.

See? My tongue trebles
over under everything
  and the viscera
you bring me
  to the tissue of
    lets me learn what's
    endurable (this

feels too much like love).

Tell me if I'm hurting you.

  OK:
    What kills is this:
    calling down
in the raised-up
        tilted-back chair

  a navel-kissing Viking
that would give the ship
  unequivocally,
  smiling, away—

  that would arch in
the layered air like a
  soldier under a
blanket hovering
  for a kiss,
a heliotrope
in the day-broken
  garden after a long,
warm night of rain.

But in your book
it's likely only
equanimity and hard-ons
that separate
aesthetes
from creeps—matters,
  in the last,
    of Form.

cloud and doorway

an iron cloud is rolling
settles to the ground as a body of
incandescent light fills an empty room
with the stuttered spinning of paper
with the animal lying down in the leaves
with matter dropping from the nutrient foliage
  the industrial thaw

she knows a little about loneliness
  it too has its moments
craving its own company
wanting the visitor to leave
so it may take her in its arms
and murmur love songs, death songs

II

II

joining the parade

a fine stretch of the inner thigh!
  people! our steps arching a city block, that's
how full my sneakers felt straddling

the harbour, an open-shirted pennant,
  grand shadow

    —then something jamming my throat
    hot star at the back of my scalp

  cross-eyed,
everything peripheral, i staggered, lay

in the median grass and waited
for the police to pass

Radius

out of

  the fluorescence to shake the rough-headed
dandelions,
back against brick, heels dug into a slope;
of course the sun's sprinkled, shattered, scintillant
skimming the green commemorative pool—fountain dor-
mant—where
far too many geese
for the good of civic order maculate
the steps with olive-black
—though there's mucoid white too—
droppings—till someone asks:
what's to be done?

an insect i couldn't name without a decade of study—i'm
down to excess now (what withal i'll never see her alien shape
again) lit on the page for a handful of seconds and then flew
off to breed or die. in the circled square, decorative railed
mandala, a pop can caught in a thermodynamic loop that,
scanning the architecture, i couldn't follow rattled back and
forth: *honggideh honggideh* it goes rolling; a mower ripping
somewhere behind us, a mechanism for growing grass, and
the bug returned and the sun on the page and the clock
tower's trapezoidal shadow. i'm out of harm's range, the
telemetry of the lens. a cook from the municipal cafeteria slips
out the back door and looking over his shoulder lights up in
the step of the sun; there's frame and shade, his shadow a
brief monument. tilted back on his heels, he's a broom leaning
against a wall at the bottom of the basement stairs.

but bicycling through Philip Morris Park, the branches in the darkness doing to skin around the ribs what breeze and over-hanging branches do, what night does filling the wooden footpath over the pond, the turning bridge lighter in the breaking foliage, my bicycle, me on it, clat-clatting around the bend: just when i thought i was happy, a girl on her knees in front of a man. he's leaning back, elbow angled on the railing, a fist in her hair. that she keeps going, that neither looks up, might extend my joy: i want to say "everything okay here, folks?" or "nice night for it," but blushing citizen, head down, pedal on.

under the lamppost i fire-up
a speckled shade of spring willow;
without these trees i'm obvious.
  a dog, breed long indeterminate,

changles jauntily by. leash slithering
behind him;

halfway around the world
villagers living too near
diamonds are losing
their hands to a machete.

mutual funds, the tv says,
are performing.

Radius: *Three Canadian diamond mining companies have been accused of fuelling the bloody civil war in Sierra Leone by providing military supplies or acting as go-between with mercenaries in order to get at the country's rich diamond resources . . . The mercenaries [Executive Outcomes Inc.] used air-burst explosives — which create and ignite a flaming vapour, burning everything and everyone within a certain radius — in their successful fight to regain control of the diamond fields.*
—Toronto, *Globe and Mail*, January 13, 2000, pages 1 and 14

Cooperman's Fish: Habitat

for the kids, of course, one fantail each:
  a standard gold, and a rock-mottled
black, foil, and amber
number—though within a week the girls
ignore them, till, months later,

  some other passing rush
of promises, and then you've four,
  an aquarium, spouting filter pump, coloured
pebbles, de-chlorinator—though you've
fended off the castle, plastic

kelp, background wallpaper of Hawaiian
sunset, and (i guess for thrash-punk
  fishkeepers) day-glo skull with eye-holes
big enough to swim through; no, half-sensible
you, it's a backyard rock, a conch

from the Cape as cover—and you're set,
  rigged for life; they're yours. to cart
the whole contraption come vacation
to the neighbours; though after time
it's not the fish

you look for, but, lying on the couch
the house asleep, dim light on a poem
or two—that steady purl; in the dead
precious silence after day, a resident gurgle

On Reading *Romantic Imperialism*

...*by the soul*
Only the Nations shall be great and free.
        —Wordsworth

O fuck if what
Makdisi says is true then everything
—no but the fundament
of what you imagined doing—is
complicit, i mean you believe(d) poetry
books are / were the *spot*
of time, healing
circle, bower within
which resistance
  vision
  celebration
  otherness become /
became the possible bloom but no

the spot of time is "doomed" as a real alternative ... precisely because it is framed
in terms of the phenomenological and cognitive space of the bourgeois subject [and]
... remains that of the individual consciousness, that of a mode of subjectivity which
is perpetually (and perhaps even structurally) at odds with its conditions of existence.

I don't deny it.

                    a tempest, a redundant energy,
                    vexing its own creation

You'll see how she attends Blake.
You'll suspend metaphor, your rattled sense

that much of what's coming's
a par-l'heure / lance game or (yet) nother form

of terr(or)torial
obs(cure)antism
—contract law for chrissake, the fine-print
of banks
 (each to its own ukulele.

  You'll reread Acorn and Souster,
   eat lunch in the camera of bus terminal
review your notes on empiricism /function
within the social order;
   you'll not love English, its itinerant grandmothers,
simply for *struthious* or *umbo*
         and   if music
matters   return.

 But for now, before the kids come home
   a spot of Victorian virtue:

         dishes, sweeping up, groceries

Teacher

It gets dark at four
now, I am talking
with the difficult boy,

and these low explicit clouds
make the sky a marble table
to stand under, our elbows

resting on the Mercury fence
that divides school from
the ravine

Here, where I can smoke and
he can swear, we explain ourselves

becoming simple, our voices
astonishingly soft

Conjugal Visit, table 16

...a man's life's no more than to say "One".
        —*Hamlet*

He's come round the silent skin
of the lake, the mercury shadow,
  rose through the ribcage,
the count of one or face
clothed in wax

He's come to June bug molecules
in terse courtship, whirring motes
insectal music
  as they sit among potted
chrysanthemums and lose an hour
or two in each other,
simply away

  A transient amnesia
let's call it, Love
still shying at the word,
  their convergence at this table
with perhaps room for something
sweet at the lips to go with coffee,
  knowing there's no setting like this
lyric they find themselves
  foreign in, how separation's
called them strangers,
that this is sometimes good

Still, the white spider
  rappelling the trellis
—glistering acrobat,

    drop of dew—
  elsewhere keeps intricacies
nets or nests, bloodmeal
carcasses for egg sacs

  There's a gnat
in her Santenay;
  her fingers, magnified, bring
it to her mouth
with an alacrity that's easy
as money, a claret-lipped
  nude kind of smiling

And cheers too to all the broken
couples they know, enduring
or getting on with it—
  and to the breeze cooling
this day-pass in which some
small word might remind them
  that they are here and why

Dove Song

i tell you again this town's going bad as an apple.
the consultants are coming, and they drive nice cars.

binocular, i perch under the flashing
await the purple blush of violence
the rose opening
  explosion of peonies, bats
over the moon, off to pollinate

  raspberries commandeer the patio
terrorist grasses outwit another chemical
the day after Ray and Cheryl tarred
the flower bed
ants made mounds of it

        so here's a crude jig,
  blood-feather purse swinging
from the new right fist:

  circling the tidal wave
    the earthquake
    the chunk of eight-lane highway
depressed like a bootprint
    in crust-snow,
  the third of me that's nothing
  for flight or grieving

  buckshot,
    bursts open like milkweed
pod, a new sun, bag of confetti
        and i'm gone

graveyard shift

some nights a sink-hole from gullet
to the plumb of his nuts
  a barrel-dumb vacancy his legs
pedal between street lights passing him
from hand to hand
  lengthening and compressing shadow

:the curb bump, halogen rectangle, Frost fence,
bike rack and brick; and Ray out for a smoke
  waving him in dog-tongued
with a masturbatory shake of imagined dice
—the upshot of yesterday's joke about
                                    Colleen

  jabbing the black button: fingers
acquitting themselves, pulling the cracked
ones from the line, or fishing out from bellies with
  a rigged coat hanger, napkins
rolled-up chip bags, the odd
dead mouse—what's left from lunches—
  bottles' lips passing
like so many o's in exclamation
bubbles, monocles,
his hands fruit-pickers or
efficient butterflies
  —bottles that have taken scores
  of kisses each: who knows how far the belt extends,
  how many mouths we've effervesced? (this
affinity once intrigued him)

  now wave upon gradual wave, sense
  webbing under the motor, belt
pulse, glass eyes:

episodes   fractal images
   songs he'd thought the years had buried
   dancing in the moonlight
   (verses and all)

   so the brain's a bucket with a hole
in the bottom. a thought a drop
   drop . . .
   a pebble in still water
drop exploding the pallet,
steam, dripping honey, the big washer's clanging,
   fork lift's efficient zip
bottles, even, their own vacancy
—though at break-bell
the smash-bin's fuller
   like pulling up home not recalling
   the drive, not one red light

John said: everyone
   needs an alternative
project: a night life I guess
they call it

project call it
plant/plant: such meanings

still mornings anticipate him,
   the wide arc; his head will
swirl in a boyhood tree canopying
the road; he'll labour
   to recall his sister's face

bottles pass, retinal burn, like soldiers in Munich

there's rain at the gate or everybody's hallucinating

Slapshot

Since the slapshot, Jean has begun considering, off and on, half-consciously, the literal possibilities of an insult her supervisor had hurled at her—the oversight costly and, admittedly, stupid—; that is, she began contemplating in her own way the consanguinity of shit and brains. Jean is freezing, pacing unevenly back and forth, smoking, one sock rolled down under the arch of one foot; the sock, a coarse industrial wool number, white-and-tawny flecked, too thick for any footwear but oversized snowboots; the sock, as well, a Valentine's gift from her ex-boyfriend who had called it (and its mate)—perhaps with the attendant imagery of a fireplace (which neither of them could claim) and Spanish coffee (which neither of them liked)—*slipper-socks*; so it's one of these socks that's not completely off now but peeled down to the instep, still covering the toes, because she'd opened the window—the air stinging, arctic—to vent the second-hand smoke that had begun to burn her eyes. It's small room, a small window, she's freezing. And the sock only partially on—her foot, she thinks, a battered naked man wearing a toque—so that the swollen ankle can breathe. It's purple, lots of purples, those astonishing bruise colours from strawberry to black, richest at the epicentre where she'd taken the slap-shot smack on the ankle bone, the round P-F Flyer bone, the tarsus. (She recalls in one limping half-traversal of the room a scramble in front of the net, clearing an opposing body from the crease; she'd lost sight of the puck well before the shot stung and felled her, rang her brain clear of instinct, the ingrained mantra for a defender: *play the man*.) After the hospital, no bone broken, she watched over the course of days as the tincture surfaced wonderfully, anticipating too, with mixed emotion, the bile pigment that would introduce, invariably, the sickly-looking but recuperative yellow; but for now the bruise is in ascension, the purples and reds deepening along the foot-length, the foot bloated like a drowned pig. Skin-tight and itchy. And swaddled deeper with each step trying her weight, the throbbing surge of blood, heart-driven, pushing itself through crushed tissue and aftershocked blood vessel, the throb seeming to draw blood from her stomach, clenching it. She doesn't know what, precisely, she is thinking as she paces the small room, cigarette between her fingers, book overturned on the desk (Lorie Moore stories); but for several seconds what registers is the faecal fist she is withholding till after she finishes the smoke, the fist compact and recalcitrant—a wrecking ball now suddenly and mightily descending, jamming against the sphincter. "Fuck off," she says. Since the slapshot, she'd been duped by it on four or five occasions, false alarms that had had her hitch herself awkwardly, pained, up the stairs, drop everything—only to strain vacuous. So now, absurdly, the shit becomes the object of revanchist sentiments and micro-manipulations typically reserved for her supervisor and more judgmental co-workers. Petty gettings-even. "You think so, eh?," she tells it, "fat chance! Not until I finish this!" She waves the cigarette—but knows acutely in her mother's voice that this is sufficient foolishness: a human being attributing conscious will to lifeless matter. But perhaps the three-day turd, sucked backed up to her abdomen like a valve-float, is indeed plotting another running start at it, or at least had begun to leach toxins into her blood that, reaching her head, made the conflation of brain and shit more plausible. What remains unclear is whether the cigarette she is, with self-satisfied defiance, pinching the turd to finish is really a laxative, inducement, stimulus finally to the very involition she would forestall until after the cigarette—enjoyed supremely if only she could shit—is ash and butted. And who can blame the turd? It's likely been dehydrated, its chamber delubricated, by the

Zylenol 3 (side effect: constipant) she'd been taking to numb, at the receptor end, the neuro-circuitry from purpling ankle to brain. This, so she can work, go to work, try to recoup the ground she'd lost after the error almost got her fired—though at night eating them indifferently, the Zylenol, for relief or recreational experiment. No the turd is only briefly the conscious object as she paces. As is the bunched-up sock under her instep. There is something else, a chiaroscuro, a phantom first cause of tonight's pacing, incessant movement, heartbeat. (No, it isn't the election results, crudely purchased; she had long been expecting that rout, had reconciled herself—with the renewed companionship of tobacco—to its structural inevitability and logic. No, it was that something, whatever it is we're lost in when, when thinking about it moments later, we've assumed we weren't thinking anything at all, the interstice between synapse and thought, how time passes unnoticed, until it, thought, the object of thought, ricochets and flashes back, as it had flashed that first night after the slapshot, flashed sudden and startling—then darted into the coral of her brain like a tropical fish. There it must have fed in remission for three impossible days, though now and then flicking its tail, naggingly, like the title of a movie of which she recalls a scene in a greenhouse and nothing more.

41

Shantung Kitsch
—notes on an osier calendar, courtesy LuckyStar Auto Repair (Markham, Ontario)

a sucker still for the willow
and the glans-headed fish

the golden froth it's leaping from
cypress moss, scaled arching of sunfall

roots erupting in the escarpment ribs
—saxifrage, on pure principle

or the persimmon its implausible hue

I'll mark the first month:

painted on willow, a willow
a man driving home in the falling snow

III

III

Mid-riff

something new from the mud of love
something growing under the fingers
something like the something I almost saw today
something like the 320-pound technician
  like the bookshelf
  like rainwater rushing to the sewer
  like the child dizzy in my arms
  the owl pellet in the bathtub drain
  like the last smoke—and I mean the *last* one
    or the foghorn canyon in a wine bottle;
  something like rehearsing for death
like intestinal bight
like today's tv massacre of the week
or the joy we wish for in moments of absent-mindedness
  something the gift-giver wants

  something like cinnamon, a red sky,
seven lean years
the embarrassed tough guy
or the girl in math class who, flicking her
jean button, laughed
  leaning back and low in her chair, bucking slightly
for the circle
of boys magnetized humming around her:

  Let's play a game and see who can give me
  the most compliments: I'll keep score till the end
  of the month!

  or the silent boy who shouted from across
the room

Glabella

I stumble into my clothes, habitual daylight
drift from one glass page to another
  What's up, Dr. Fish? Can you kiss
  yourself on the mouth?
      (*Op Op Op*

Last weekend, her arms, hands,
  broad holy words.
Here's wonder, they said, slipping
through the trapezoidal sunlight
(crane swooping over grass)

  then extricated her hair
from the collar of a sweater
  then removed the sweater

  In the pitch winter
  woken to alarm
  i walk through the blood
  meet the hearth-warmed dog
  at the body's centre

    almost happy
  thin as a razor, whole
  and immense as a bean

For months

the sky'd been a waiter
  smog-worn rag over his forearm
every section smoking; we waited
by the refinery. then a stunning
cloud bank strolled in,
my love and i ordered the flaming fountain
  drank it quickly, rushed off to the woods

the birds as soon as we began,
the husking dreys, stopped talking

She in her garden,

pentamerous and frost-gloved
what's a word to a kiss?
   depends on the word
   depends on the kiss
   depends on how still the crow's stare—
quale! quale! quale! :the worm's extended
itself on the branch it emulates
   breached in its vagile hug

   (huge urge
   it's not love we learn by rote
   rhyme rides a horse
   said the goat

Bon soir Monsieur Monster

it's nothing, she murmured
just a June obituary

wind shaking the ament
sound wanting content
(her elbow most eloquent

Lori, as postcard

gesture written into the weather
into the eye of memory
that butterfly, something like you in the geode
of the street, high latex boots
the falling light you're angled in making
blue spikes of rain, studded drops
on your plastic skirt

against night's cigarette
longitude and leg, classic:
death, breath, leg, smoke

i remember how your growing into beauty once startled and emblazoned you

Blue Jets

She takes blessedly
Giving with full hands.
    —Milton Acorn

Thirteen, bored and giddy
with our maleness
we'd sit around some
summer evenings, cock our asses
in the air, brace back our
  thighs with our forearms,
  strike the match
  hold it there, and let fly
the incendiary fart: Ka-
  boom!

boys boys boys

  hilarity, the brute puissance,
  Apollo 11-ish,
of the blue spurt shooting
from our very own holes
  flaring along the perineum
(the blunt sandpaper landing-strip
that begins under the testicles
  and terminates darkly at the anus,
that place)—

  the flame riding the mid-seam
of our jeans, sputtering beads
if the flatus dribbled,
  the burnt-fingered diminuendo
of the dud—*who knows what lurks?*

or fanning shockingly out
  if rich and deeply baffled
the trapped blast, supernova,
  combusting in the grotto then spreading
like wings from our thighs
like violets
so we'd have to beat
it back: stop drop and roll.

  Later, I'd grin learning
the blue jet was very like
what Hamlet meant
by *hoist by their own petard*—it would
all come back to me

but for now, for then: for the girls
  who over the span of summers
  let us kiss and feel them
    in the incest of cottage
rotations, neat eclipses of
  the X-ed calendar, another August's
early darkening,

it confirmed us: *demented*
  immature and *gross*

just what we needed from them
—antidote to the top-forty love songs
they sang soulfully as dumkas,
arms linked, weaving with flashlights
down gravel roads
as we, twenty paces back,
  practiced walking and pissing
at the same time

Stairwell

quickly, we haven't
time for proof, to say

nothing of language or the
symmetry of our scaled wings

fucking around

Fess up, said the bull—
I was squaring myself twenty
paces back holding out the cape
(a worn red sweater, really)
at arm's length, my fingers
clothes-pegs; was ginger
too in holding my nerve
   —*There's a more profound humanity*
in any drinking hole, you've nothing
to float a stone. Watch out!
   Here comes pain.

        Still, for a moment
I was sequined in the ring;
swans were swarming, explosive
   horseflies; pruinose bones
spun like cartoon stars
   above a dazed David
   —beyond deciding,
a caesura, dust
   sifting the spike of sunlight

   That was the very blink
he needed; red-eyed, el toro
came hoofing it,
   and head-on too:
   I turned tail, hands
over my flapping culet

   A knock at the door,
Liz pokes in her head:
   It's time to kiss

the kids goodnight
    she's wearing a fine-fitting
sweater, the fleeting glare /
    patient exasperation
of an overworked woman married
to a fool (who's in love with her

but poorly). *What are you doing?* she asks
    eyeing the grey drops
plink-plonking
    from the ceiling tiles
into our best aluminum cooking pot

    Nothing Love just
fucking around

    and in the backdraft
of the closed door I am upside down,
keister-blooded but covered
    in her kisses, flying
    over the burladero, the crêpe-
festooned balustrade, over the second
row bleachers

and fat onto the deposed
    emperor's lap

Neighbour

you leap onto the porch
and mocking immortality turn
to smoke
　　　—John B. Lee

She strays, bow-throated,
a bowl in each hand
into morning's diffusion
scans back hedge-shadows
the yard scattered with shreds
　of newspaper, spoor, margarine
tubs counting drizzle

　—steps bent and mewing in cloth
coat and fur-collared boots
　steps small and wide-hipped
　a creeping frigate.

　　:Hey Nellie, where'd you hide the sun?
　　:Satyr's not come home yet.
　　:Oh.
　　　　Which one's he again?

She plants her face
on the fencetop, brings me
like the plate of Christmas cookies
　a piece of her secret work.

And Marty, a brilliant homespun
nihilist who'd routinely gut me
　at chess,
wandered Riverdale for a month
　after his cat went missing.

I held my tongue.
One morning, black-eyed, he said: *She's dead somewhere.*

And Nellie had told me
   If you listen closely, cats
   tell you their names.

Now, in the sog, it's Satyr's back-story;
we're all royalty, white moth.

A dog-man, I nod anyway.
The rain falls in angles.

extra help

of course she's brilliant
talented young
and like most of her friends
wears a jacket in class
      (hers a silver pillowy space thing
for the unpredictable thermostat
or quick egression for a between-class
smoke

now in the quiet, just the two of them
the room's huge, and halfway through
Layton's *If I Lie Still*
getting at the subjunctive,
the speculative big *If*
the same one in Williams' *Dance Russe*
she shoulders herself out
of the jacket, smiling—
the revelation a cotton terror

it's not till the end, door still open,
the *Thanks, that helps a lot*

that he contextualizes the tight
bud of her nipples, cold
or appreciative or against
all will and reason
complimentary

so many ways that love makes victims
she knows the blood and sings it
without rehearsal

the fluorescent lighting's
  a chorus of flies

:this is for those who have stolen plums

IV

A dragonfly

dying under a lawn chair
is a proposition
  woken from pupal
duplicity, ancestral egg

again (fuck it): things are
  what they
touch—the body's
a shuddering, a fragment
  (this is sunlight

or the wind's brittle fingers
in the grass

pushing in the grocery line

and it's all fine, a tight thursday, till the sudden
opening of a new register—that, and our standing
elbow-to-elbow from the free lane, me and the black-
draped crow, end-of-the-week hag whose brain's
some feral abacus clicking:
　　the number of carts in each line
　　the number of items per basket
　　the relative efficiency of sandy or k.c.
or jean. *can i help the next in line, please?*
yeah, and i'm out first with a head-fake
or maybe she is
　　anyway, it's started: our steps
quicken like those skittering xylophonic
birds', sandpipers; open coats, carts
rattling, a bit of the hip as we log-jam
cater-corner at the chocolate and tabloid rack.
　　and here's adept thickness! her flummery
jaw set fierce, eyes stone cold
to my gritted nods and smiles,
my begged sardonic pardon and inching
basket of steel—but she's nudging
too! staring clear through me
staring through and leaning hard
so that but for the force of her in my wrists
and forearms i know what it means
to be invisible.
　　do you laugh or swat her,
take her by the throat or in your arms?
i'm seeing turn-of-the-century furrows, ox cart
tracks thick in the mud, potatoes,
a sandy-haired farm boy crazy
with wonder for the strength of her kiss

—that boy running home, swinging his arms
wide at the scend of an open blue hill
trying to fly because of her.
have i kissed the crone, her tongue
like moss? *Baba-Yaga!!*
here's yelling, confusion, people:
  and outside a rush-hour horn blast
and the sudden-cold darkness coming fast

An odd invisibility, this

On the staff corkboard someone'd tacked
  a personals ad: *Kittens Need a Home*
  (large felt heading, soft-lit
polaroid of kitten in classic mid-back-roll,
  paws frozen in classic mid-swipe at classic
cat toy—a belled cloth mouse)
  and under this:
  I'm thoroughly irresistible
  must spoil me with love

and so on

Phyllis and them—I knew it—
  small, fist-faced termagants or,
con/versely, women of unfathomable
seismic passion;
  they sit at any rate
smoking at the math table
  with Claire Winston, who
first class each term counts
leather jackets in the back row
and numbers their days,
actually says squinting:. . . *and period three—*
  six leather jackets! I give them a week.
  Kids call her "The Terminator";
the math dysfunctional
especially males, something like
  hate her
  but I'll grant this:
each Halloween she does it up full
  tilt as a witch.

But watch them go ape-shit at
  Christmas!
these women with extra-big
December issues of *Cat Fancier*
  or catalogues of cat stuff
ailurophile paraphernalia,
ribbons, strange largesse,
photo album exchanges of plum-sized
hearts—their own framed in
  endearing or dignified poses
  some on pedestals,
long-stemmed bouquets
or murky blue depths-of-field
in the background
—professional portrait photography
is what I'm saying.

   Kittens need a home.
  Okay, it's a humanizing thing.
   But how could I not scrawl
between photocopies of Stilt Jack
and Layton
glancing over my shoulder
—each flash a detonation—

  faking the high road or struck
impatient with human misery: *How about*

a canvas bag and a lake?

Giddap, News Boy
—the Slough

i. Come butterfly song

   dream-flying man
   Come affiliate lyric
pendulum-scythe, constellation of lichen
  scabbing the stone wall:
at your foot the mass of butchered
are flute-song, peat and smoke

Come fruit-song then
—imago from a sleeping bag,
short-winged fly from the corpse
of a peach:
we're halfway sentient
absurd alarmed at one boy's famine
  the plum of bruise on a woman's cheek

(no, love-shorn and fugitive it began truly,
  he'd shot north-west, chased a cut
  of headlight through mountainous collapse
   blasted granite marquees

      Todd + Loraine 4 ever
      Rock Machine

while over the radio, oceans away
a poet proclaimed in blood
  this erumpent fig
   that damselfly's

hesitation

ii.   Allula hallelujah

Once a chat-bird, patient sensei
instructed him: *You too! You too!*

he was careless singing, that's
what the wingbeat said:
sing as if you're already home

iii.   White-sheathed lyric stubborn under the wing

   he hikes it humbly (humbly humbly) back to the slough
and there crouched naked on a boulder
   sketches the twin ramifications
   of a fallen fir
moss-dressed—and beside that
   an infant island no wider than
   a bar stool
     holding three
   species of new tree:
     goose sedge and other brush
   whose roots, rhizomes (i guess
        are setting
        will stay
        harness a silt bed

   or be eaten when the trail
   beside the acid lake, isthmus
   shored with rocks

   is picked apart by a hard season
   and not thought worth the traffic to re-stone

     there's no way back from here
     the birds have eaten all the crumbs . . .

iv.   O Forest Manager, o fig!
   we're barefoot in it now, the slough:

shin-deep in love cloud and carbon,
  held between two skies,
 our most loyal excuse
best cleverness
 ardent touch of the lips
scat of asters and bees we've eaten

 become microbic spasms—and the sun
a silver bug
 swallowed by a fish.

    a planet give or take
   (you knew all this beginning,

 standing ever-cousin to a fern
i mean i meant its twinging
 flagellated sperm

Fail

okay: something a student,

Gabriella, tells him in the library, well after her diminutive
beauty, reluctant return to the antidepressants they talked
about in the hall as the VP tapped his foot for one of them.
early on she'd met him after class, established things: *Really
Sir I cry so easily, I can't take anything even a little disturbing.* she
sits out *Welcome to Sarajevo*, takes Neruda—Tarn's bilingual
edition—to the library; racks up absences tending her sister's
little boy, the credit a wash-out he'll account for in a memo.

I dreamed you were my boyfriend's father—he stands struck
by her animation, a little late for class, the new semester.
*We are at your house, the three of us in your kitchen. It's very
clean and you're tossing a salad. You'd made chicken because
you didn't know I was a vegetarian, but when I tell you, you
don't freak out or anything, you just keep tossing the salad. And
the lettuce leaves are falling in a kind of slow motion, they're SO
green; it was a good dream, Sir.*

chroma

the sun's a one-line poem
the blade of grass a girl i've known
i awoke gasping (in a nursing home

no no, we're naked in a field,
the hand-picked glass books we'd lent each other
(annotations berry-red and contrary) tossed
to the scrub with our underthings

what crabbed signature bedded me here?
what hammer-hearted daughter?
the weevil in the ripening bole
has much, still, to countermand:

in the bloom of dark, full sweeping night
an open-throated moon made us a bending
readiness

i haven't fallen in love this week;
that's cold plenty, and you, i keep

returning
a man to a tv show
bee to anther
waking to digital clock
limina to song
(boy to the pond

then suddenly here at pistol-point
our hands folded behind our heads
kneeling in a meadow

Consolation

She's thirsty, there's a bird
near the window, a headlight,
her tongue hurts;

  or maybe it's what she told me
springing up after I'd tried
  for the nth time to tuck
her in:
  I can't believe I'm
alive and in the world!

  Now another nightmare standing
  by the bed, third night
in a row—my side, I'm
the easier mark—
  a shadow I've come grumbling to
from eddies of half-
remembered touch

      to walk her again
through the rim
of the bathroom night light
  her voice taking consolation
    me, counting the hours
till work, the dead slog
of the body brittle
  by noon

and when the dinosaur laughed in a kind of evil
voice "I'm not your grandmother" it scared me,
I can't get it out of my head

Think of snow, I say, the dream
  talked out, lying with her
  holding her and spinning
out the image,
  half the world asleep,
    Five more minutes

(But the inconclusiveness
of child-rearing sciences,
  the authenticity
of need, when we should sleep
alone—thirty-five's
a good number—and other
stubborn catechisms of the heart

  —these rise up when, as I dislodge
my arm, she grabs me
round the neck, fiercely,
  pleading still as I pry away
  her fingers

  She's whimpering now in the
next room, will
  quiet herself
  I think

  rehearsing for loneliness,
  growing a space to hold
the widening red pool (call
it loss or longing
  —*Love despises the desperate*—or hours
  she'll lie awake
back to back with a man

She's stopped calling; I'm up;
Laura, supine, is snoring like a dinosaur

and everything umbral in a kind of mute
study, I circle her sleeping nipple
with my thumb

Invisible Hands

The cost of a stock option is the difference between the amount received by the company when the option is exercised and the greater amount that the company could have received if the shares had been issued at the market price. This cost never appears on the income statement. Under a phantom plan, the amount equal to the increase in the market price . . .
   —R.B. Matthews, President of Manitou Capital Corporation

It is a general hypnosis.
   —Anton Chekhov

some people make strange money
some people make strange money

i met an old friend proud
 of his eight-
thousand dollar watch, car
at ninety-six grand—cockades,
 i suppose, for magnates
 or the pert young captains
of leverage

 it's tinsel to tell time,
feed villages! i nearly
 yelled (but wary
of sanctimony instead
leaned in and kissed
 his ear: *what multitudes!*
it's time (all we're in)

 —a reprieve from the needles
and threads of living
 lives as bent pins,

from mops through cabinet
windows of office towers
at three a.m.

from faggots on the shoulder
 fingers on the stalk
on the stem

 the asphyxiated leaf

 $

some people make strange money
some people make strange money

 parliaments bankrolled

by people who etcetera etcetera
by incorporated paper bodies

suspend
this car jewel frippery
 as the engine
of the blue century

 some people,
 their ab-
stracted digits clicking
 in the phantom language
of interest
 (more confounding
 even than poetry
 or love

make strange money
  tell the poor they're damn lucky
  lecture the poor about laziness
                             excess
                             responsiblity

(and at banquets tax-broken
  under Cayman palms
  again rewire the structures
  to their own premium

soft money
hard earth

oilfields' black billowing
the tumescent, self-immunizing tomato

Ipperwash and the Ontario Provincial Police

Ipperwash/Aazoodhena: selected notes

The non-violent management of conflict is the very essence of democracy.
    —Kofi Annan

i. Provincial officials have refused to confirm or deny that just before the fatal shooting of an aboriginal protester at Ipperwash Provincial Park [Aazhoodena] in 1995, someone at a high-level government meeting urged the OPP to "get the [expletive] Indians out of the park even if you have to use your weapons". . . .It [the provincial government] also refused to confirm or deny that someone at the meeting ridiculed a suggestion to negotiate an end to the occupation at Ipperwash Provincial Park [Aazhoodena]. After the shooting, Premier Mike Harris denied that he or his cabinet ministers were involved in the decision to use force on the protesters. He maintained that it was entirely a police decision. A spokesman for the Attorney-General's Ministry said . . . the government "will make disclosures of documents and participate in examinations for discovery in the ordinary course, at the appropriate time."

ii. The Ontario Solicitor-General's Ministry has not destroyed any relevant records relating to the aboriginal occupation of Ipperwash Provincial Park [Aazhoodena] in 1995, according to Solicitor-General Jim Flaherty.

iii. Computer records compiled by a police officer who helped plan the provincial government's response to the native occupation of Ipperwash Provincial Park [Aazhoodena] have been purged, according to a sworn affidavit by the province's deputy solicitor-general. The missing records are the first official indication that documents about Ipperwash [Aazhoodena] . . . may no longer be available. The electronic files, compiled by Ontario Provincial Police Superintendent Ron Fox, were sought . . . under the *Freedom of Information Act*.

iv. Protesters said the land contained a sacred burial ground, an argument later upheld by a federal court. . . . [Acting Sergeant] Kenneth Deane was given a two-year suspended sentence and ordered to perform 180 hours of community service. . . .The court had heard that Deane fired seven shots from his sub-machinegun the night [Dudley] George was killed. Three shots were at George, while four shots, which missed, were directed at other Indian protestors. . . . [Judge Hugh] Fraser found that Deane lied when he testified that he saw George holding a rifle. . . .Fraser told the court there was no evidence that any of the protesters were armed.

i. from "Province tightlipped on Indian clash," *Globe and Mail*, December 4, 1996

ii. from "Records Preserved: Ministry," *Globe and Mail*, June 24, 1998

iii. from "Ipperwash incident records missing," *Globe and Mail*, September 17, 1998

iv. from "Court upholds conviction of OPP officer in shooting," *Toronto Star*, February 19, 2000

Nose to The Rosebud With High-minded Seriousness

You could golf with King Canute

    but which one?
   There were three
   clustered around the tenth
century, round and round
the North Sea

You'll make it
  a foursome, then
you and three King Canutes;
   spotting each other
kibitzing
splashing your irons
into sand traps
   drinking root beer
and naming laws
of succession
until, between your
shadows and the last little
flag, the sun rolls
behind a hill

little life

speaking with the one good eye
they made clear through wading
in terminal gardens. here's attention
to forsythia and bentwood grass,
a tended balance, bamboo set off
  behind the fountain—a mound
of mortared rock whose rubber tube
they're always adjusting
  so the water-sounds
fall just right.
              and cicadas
  a kind of locust, really,
    calling in the summer's last poem

Talk Me Out of It

Talk baby talk to me, my baby
  talk baby talk to me
that irrefutable bantling
gabble
that sweeps the world
away and says *there is only*
  us in
our infancy

that tonight no hunger swells
  no woman cries on the lip
of a wound or leaves
her child to freeze in a field
  —that no student buckles under
  a pistol butt,
    no middleman takes
his cut in blood
  (and all that other
metastasis our shiny bodies
  would reprieve
tap dancing amazement after
  amazement on the stage of our
radiant skins that underneath know
the long ellipses—how we
  mouth fiercely
catching our breath, bucking
the seditious pulsion
    'cause we can't really be here
  and not take the bastards
  to heart.

Look, parliament's
 bought and bolted;

we're sleepwalking in an image

 but that MTT plant's
still sitting in Sarnia, nobody's
home there now, and I've a book
of matches: let's kiss

MTT (methylcyclopentadienyl manganese tricarbonyl) and Canadian Sovereignty under NAFTA: "In the resulting deal, Ottawa agreed to ... pay 13 million (U.S) to Ethyl [of Richmond, Va.] in damages and provide an admission-that there is no scientific evidence ... that MTT interferes with emission-control equipment or poses a health-risk. In return, Ethyl dropped all trade and court cases. Ottawa issued the statement despite increasing-evidence that low-level exposure to airborne manganese is linked to nervous-system problems and attention deficit disorder in children."
    —Toronto, *Globe and Mail*, July 24, 1998

Notes:

On Reading *Romantic Imperialism*

i) Makdisi, Saree, *Romantic Imperialism* (Cambridge University Press, 1998)

ii) the italicized chunk on the first page from the Makdisi text

iii) "a tempest..." is from Wordsworth's "Prelude, Book One."

Graveyard Shift

"drop ... a pebble ...": pinched from a guy I took a workshop with at University of Florida twenty-plus years ago.

Giddap, News Boy

"there's no way back from here ... crumbs": David Bromberg, "Last Song for Shelby Jean," in *David Bromberg*, (Columbia Records)